I0442266

Big Cats Coloring Book

Realistic Adult Coloring Book, Advanced Animals Coloring Book for Adults

by Amanda Davenport

Realistic Animals Coloring Book: Vol 7

ISBN-13: 978-1530715213

ISBN-10: 1530715210

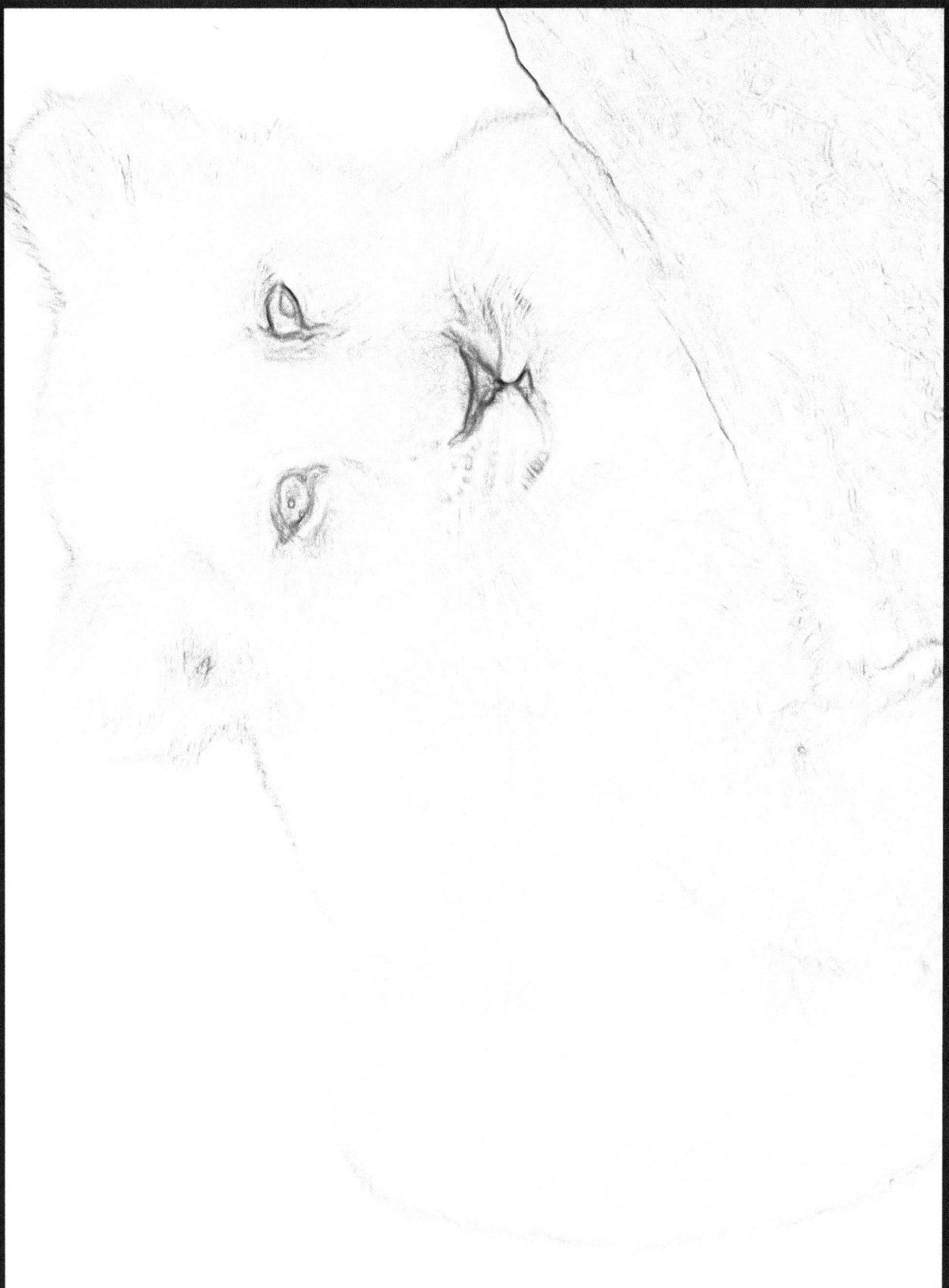

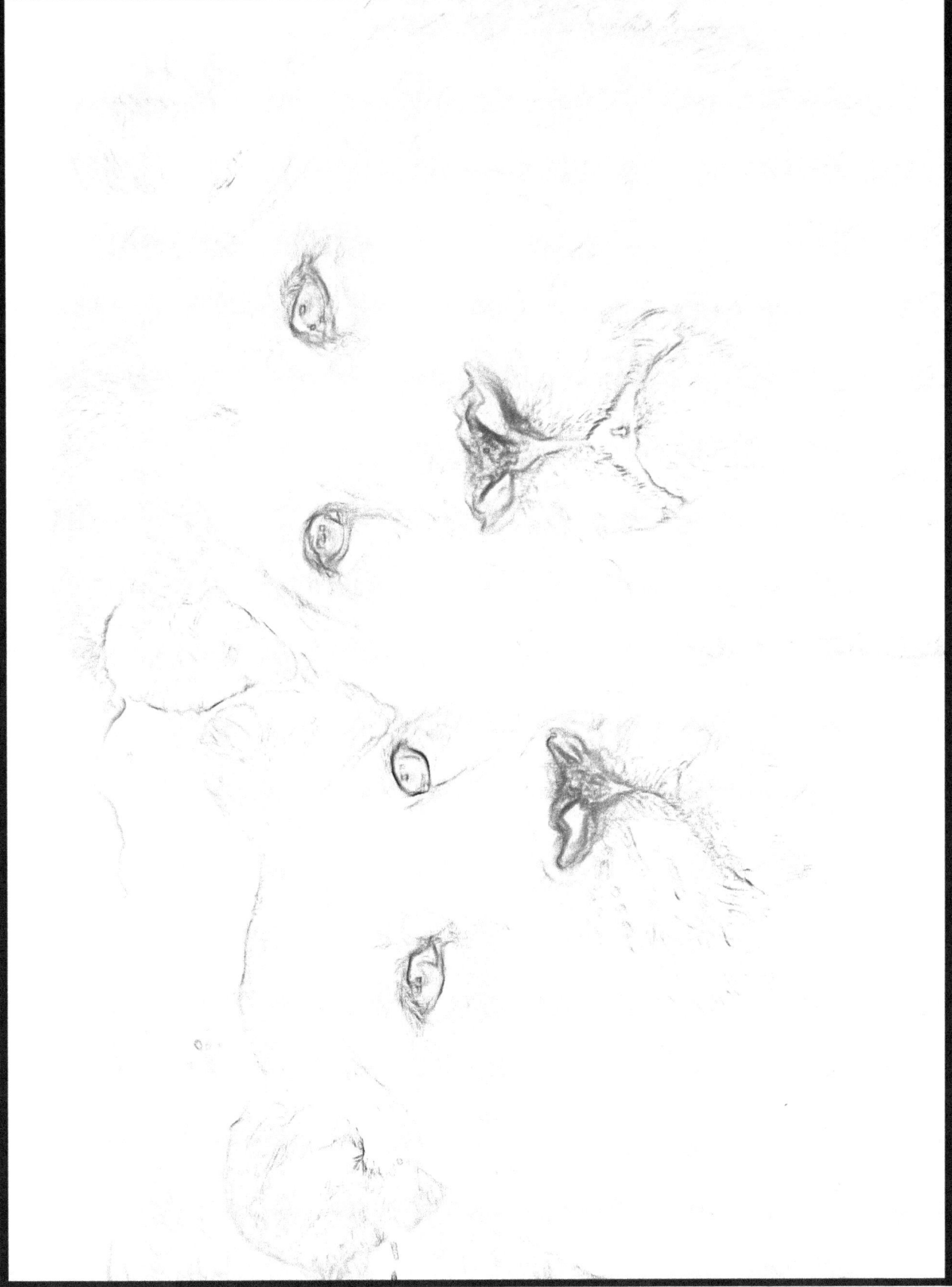

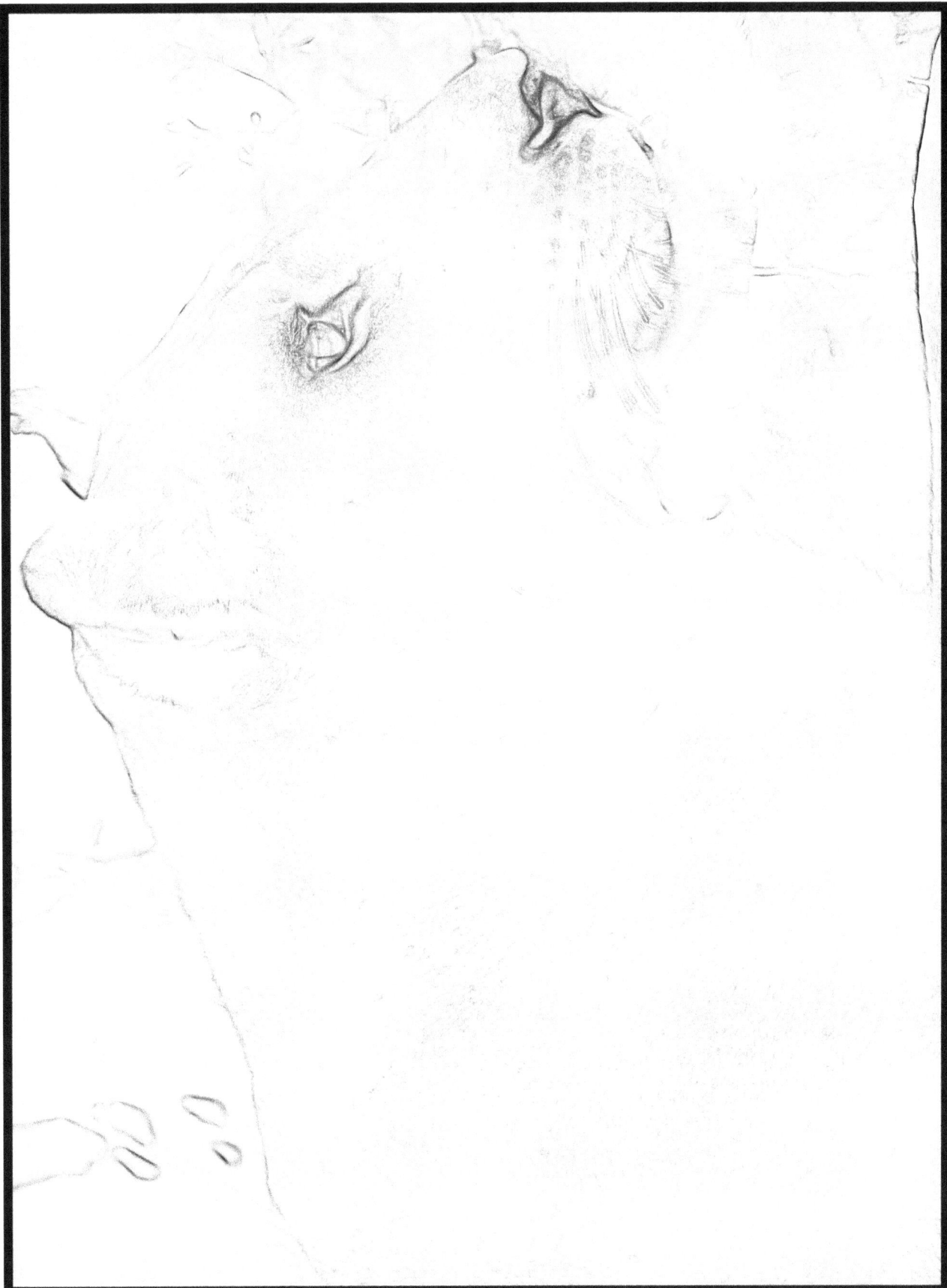

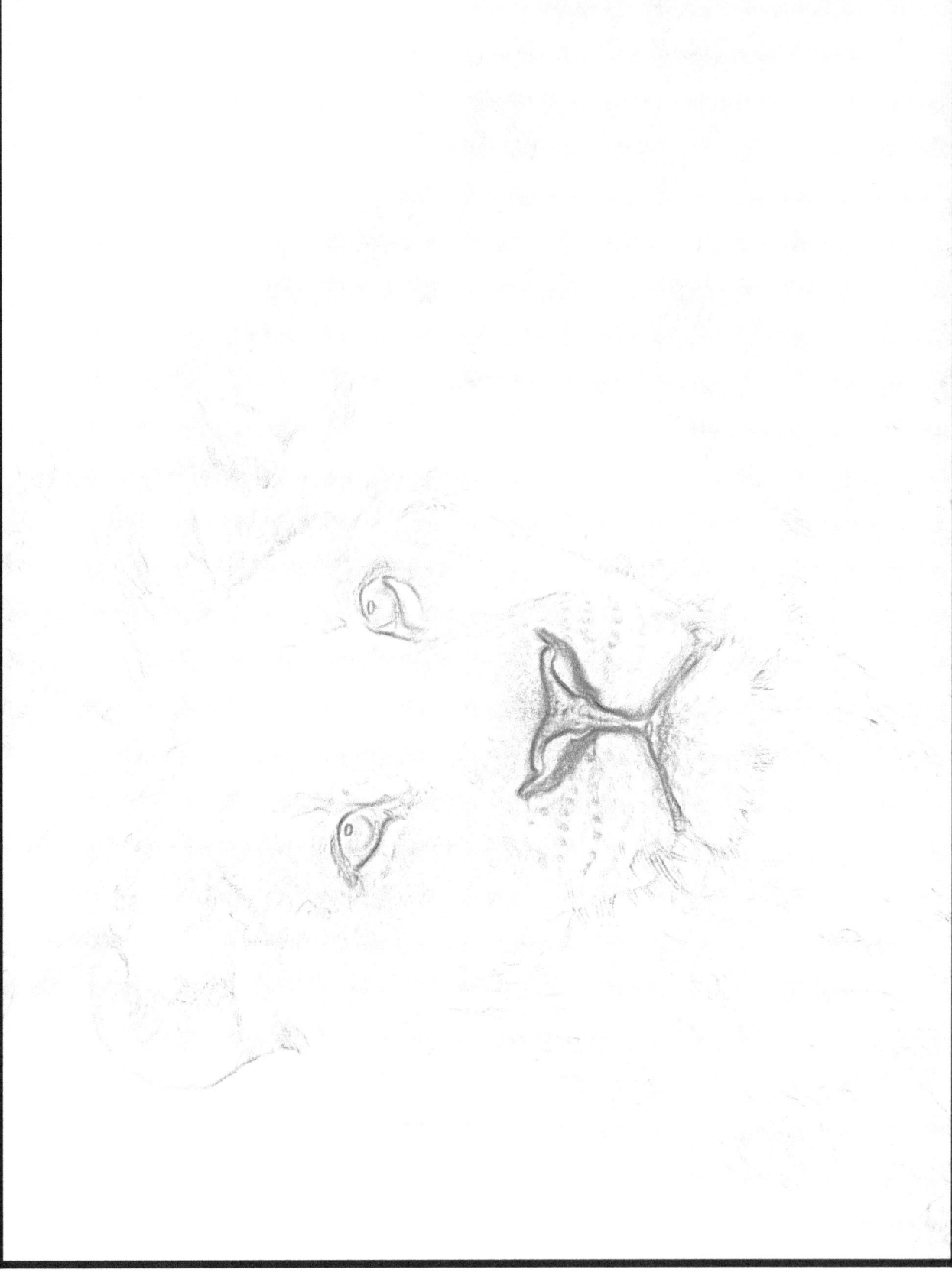

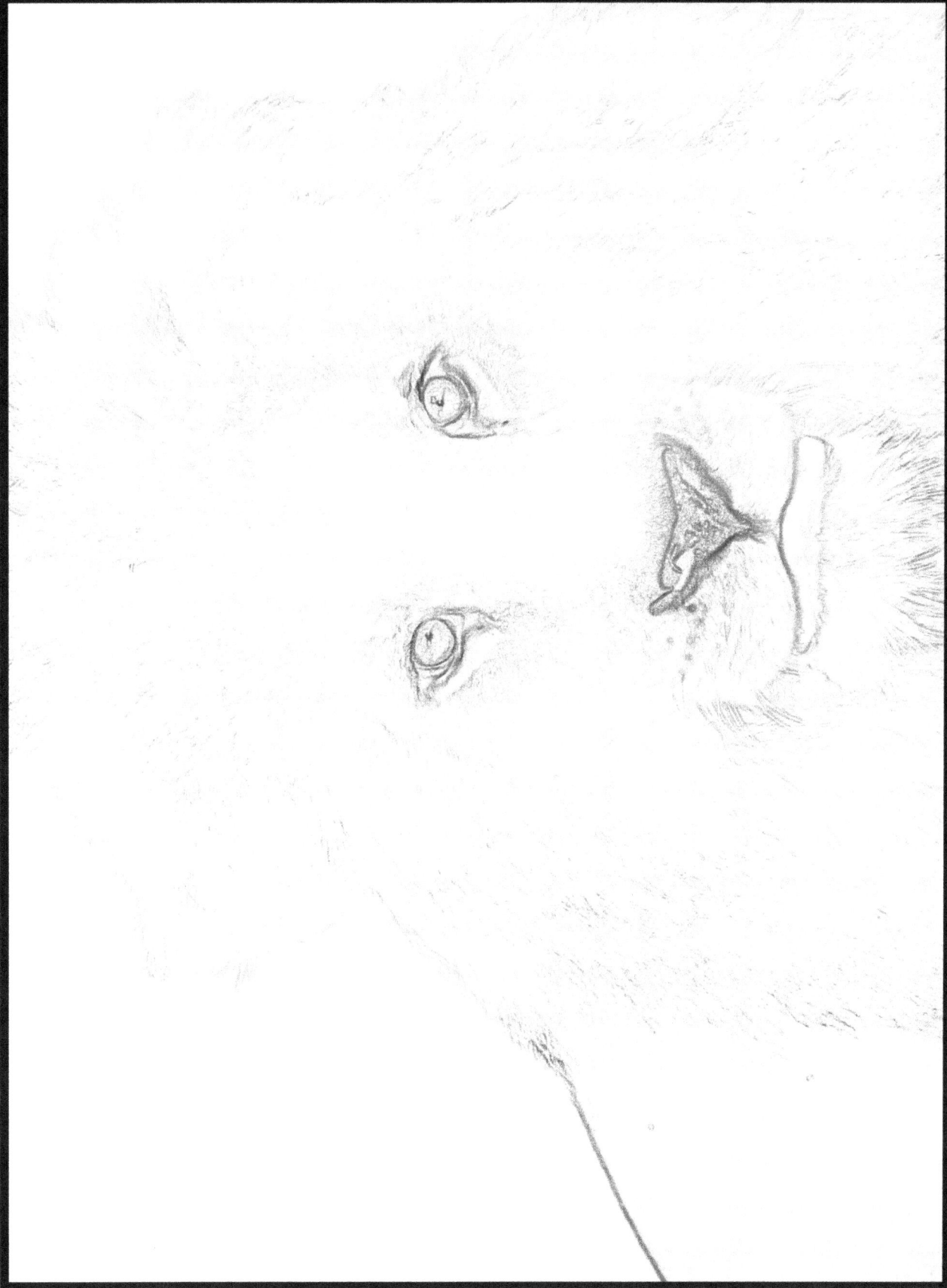